THIRD
HAND
BOOKS

Where to begin? That this book is a knockout? Check. That the voice of Gion Davis is compelling and constantly pushing the edge of thinking into a new understanding of being? Check. Here is one of the many ambitions of this remarkable book: "I wanted / to write something / so full it felt empty, / an ornate bowl from the past / filled with nothing / but what happened." And what happens here in *Designated Stranger* is the absolute now of struggling to remain sovereign in a broken nation. It's a road book, a diary, a love letter, a treatise on an abject Americana. Let me finish where I began, this book is a knockout.

– PETER GIZZI, author of *Fierce Elegy* and *Now It's Dark*

If Jack Kerouac had been a trans man in contemporary America "with no job and a credit card" raised on a sheep ranch in rural Española, New Mexico, writing unstanzaed poems that ribbon vertically down the page like rattlesnakes, he might have created something like Gion Davis's *Designated Stranger*, an of-the-moment but timeless, Beat-style masterwork. The brilliance of these poems is inseparable from their bravado and bravery, their eye for the truth and their eye for the truth of glorious details: the "agate alien eyes / of bighorn ewes," "a Northern Harrier // flying low over the Dollar Tree," "the veal kennels / Backlit on the hills with little steers silhouetted inside them." I love Davis's mordant humor in the face of pain, delivered in full poker face: Life is a "bad idea in cowboy boots." "When I remember the old life, it's the way bubblegum / remembers an extinct banana." "Body, a pegboard / to hang anger on / beside the hammers / in the garage." It is difficult to explain and even more difficult to render "queer effervescence" at it appears in rural places. For those of us raised where "even the real flowers looked plastic," we designated strangers, well, we know it when we see it.

– DIANE SEUSS, author of *frank: sonnets* and *Modern Poetry*

Rising tender from the ashes of American Romanticism, Gion Davis's *Designated Stranger* exhibits a polyphony of forms, insights, and attitudes anybody with a soul still online in their brains might use to remember how to breathe. "Who will / Read my poems when everyone is dead?"

Davis asks, foreboding of a life measured by wandering still-yet-to-be-had even after we've been broken and rebuilt so many times we hardly hold form. One thing's for sure: Gion Davis refuses to give up on his best ghosts, whether we deserve their candor or not, and his continuing bravura for revitalizing longing from neck-deep in the undead is a line in the sand I'll hold like a candle.

– BLAKE BUTLER, author of *Molly*

I'm not sure I can accurately explain why or even pinpoint exactly when, but at a certain point in reading *Designated Stranger,* I realized I was crying. I think it's the way the sadness tangles up in knots with how beautiful it all is—the world I mean, but also the poetry. I think it's the fact that they're so inextricably linked. That we have to have both—the vast emptiness that comes with being human, and the unrepentant joy that comes with counting the flower bushes and the blackbirds and the truck-stop diners. Gion carries it to us, all somehow contained in his hands alone, and lets us pull threads until we find the piece we need.

– DAN CAMPBELL, lead singer and songwriter for The Wonder Years

Joy does not come cheap in *Designated Stranger*. America makes nothing easy. No one consents to being born in a place requiring credit scores, and Davis lyricizes economic precarity, gender expansion, and a turbulent family of origin with convincing buoyancy. Despair could easily flatten these intersections, but poem after poem—with quotables galore—Davis writes odes to life that include the world and all its particularities.

– K. IVER, author of *Short Film*

Thirdhand Books LLC, Logan, UT 84321
www.3rdhandbooks.com
© 2026 by Thirdhand Books
All rights reserved.
Printed in the United States of America

Library of Congress Cataloging-in-Publication Data on File

ISBN (paperback): 978-1-949344-67-7
1 2 3 4 5

Front cover image: Madeline Rupard, *Right Before Therapy* (2021)

Cover design by Lindsey Webb.

DESIGNATED STRANGER

Gion Davis

Thirdhand Books
Logan, Utah
3rdhandbooks.com

Contents

"What does it mean, American?

It means, mostly, to go unnoticed, to watch the streets filling with crowds, & then
To step into the crowd, to be it suddenly, to type behind a desk all day where no one
Sees you. To conceal all that you are. To perform your whole life in a silence

As deep as any girlhood is; to brim over like a black pond in summer & say nothing
about it."

— Larry Levis, *The Widening Spell of Leaves*

"God have mercy on the man who doubts what he's sure of."

— Bruce Springsteen, *Tunnel of Love*

The Thing No One Wants You to Know

You can actually run away. You are allowed to go, at least for a little while. You can drive all over the place and end up in California and eat fried cod in Fort Bragg and half-joke about moving there even though you know you won't because small towns you can only get to by wild little highways aren't really your thing anymore.

You are allowed to have the most perfect day you can remember, even though you are tired from sleeping on an inflatable mattress in some stranger's living room. It'll be a day where it doesn't matter that you are trans, that you are newly twenty-eight, that you are waiting on the hospital bill from your boyfriend having to go to the ER with COVID after you lost your insurance because you quit your job three weeks ago to run off into the country.

It won't matter that you're a poet standing under some giant redwoods and wondering if they ever have perfect days and what those days are like. Maybe just the right amount of sun, just the right amount of rain, just the right amount of passing nutrients back and forth to one another underground in secret. It's hard to imagine anything going wrong for them. I stood in the burned-out heart of a tree that was still healthy and enormous everywhere except right at the bottom in the middle which was empty. You could have lived inside it. Maybe someone has.

The rest of the west is so dry and sick. The trees in Montana are brittle and yellow. The fire scars jumping the road in Washington. The blown-down timber like shiny dog hair in southern Oregon. In Wyoming, there are no trees and it rained all night long. Lightning spread its fingers out for miles across the sky, firing like cannons right over the van, and we laughed because there was nothing else to do but hope for the best.

Remembering how rapidly things can change while you are in the narrow stripe of redwoods still standing in Humboldt County feels ridiculous.

You lie on your back in the shamrocks and ferns and watch the blue jays darting hundreds of feet up from tree to tree, and the threads of spiderwebs, and little needles falling silver in the breeze, and wonder if any of your life even exists outside of today in California. If anyone even remembers or cares and if you care if they do or not. And then you'll wander down to where a river that is even shallower and narrower than the Rio Grande is limping along even though its bed is easily a thousand feet wide and you'll pick through the toxic algae with your boys to skip rocks.

I think the thing about the redwoods is they are like the ocean in their intense indifference. But unlike the ocean they are individually alive like you are, sort of, maybe. I don't know if you've ever noticed but they hum in the wind the way a cave might hum. The breeze never touches the forest floor but they are so tall that, up high, the wind is fast and it resonates all the way down.

Adam broke a bunch of reeds off by the river and whistled through them like a pan flute while we asked Alec, who has perfect pitch, what note it was (somewhere between a G and an F). And we got back in the van and drove down the 1, which is a road that twists through the woods like a loose shoelace in a way that makes you consider how many trees were cut down to make this stupid road in the first place—just for what? Something to look at? But then you burst out of the forest onto the ocean and you're like *oh fuck holy shit this fucking road man this is it this is America this is what learning to drive a car is fucking all about.* And the ocean is turquoise blue with black rocks and black sand and black pelicans and the fog on the coast is opalescent white and you take a bunch of goofy pictures and videos because you're so relieved to be done driving the fucking 1 through the woods like that. But you are also five friends who are all a little in love, because that's what touring with a band is like, so you hug a lot and hold onto each other and climb up on the guardrail and the top of the van, and it is tender and silly and precious.

And then you drive to Fort Bragg and go down to the wharf and get a pilsner and fish and fries and Mike makes Alec laugh harder than you've ever seen him laugh while you sit by the water feeling so good and so free because you haven't even thought about your email for a week. I could say a hundred bitter things about transphobia across the country and hippies and broken vans and broken hearts but today, today was so perfect it was like nothing has ever gone wrong.

If Larry Levis said, "My life has no witness / When I whisper to myself," and Lisa Jarnot said, "I am loving you beside the man with his pants down on / the highway where you are love itself and dying," and you and Riley and Alec joke about getting matching tattoos in Reno of Frank O'Hara saying, "you / wet your pants and I'll wet mine," then what else? It's only been since you've started doing the impossible that this secret trapdoor in reality has opened.

There is profundity in diminishing returns, in knowing if you went back with all the same people at the same time next year, it wouldn't be the same. The restaurants that don't feel as fun the second time you're there. The people who get older, more complicated, less joyful. The fires that eat up the trees and the floods that wipe away bridges. It is getting smaller, this world we know best. And, in that shrinking, there is also permission.

You'll get to your cowboy-themed motel in Willits after driving up from the ocean at sunset while the trees and the fog and the mountains and the canyons dripped golden with the weight of late August. You'll walk to the gas station across the street to buy beer and a church key with Adam, whose bed is too short or whose legs are too long. The feeling that has been skulking around the horizon all day, the one that reminds you that you may never see the redwoods again, sits doglike by the door, waiting.

I am not going to live for a thousand years. I am not a redwood tree or a deep-sea sponge. I am a twenty-eight-year-old trans guy with no job and a credit card who is surprised to still be alive at all.

I think the thing they don't want you to know about transness is it frightens others because, at a certain point, there is a moment where you think to yourself, "I can't do this anymore." And then you don't. You give up. You leave because staying would be impossible. It isn't brave, it's fleeing into the hollow forest of your heart to find the life you've come to realize you've missed so much of while pretending to want something else. You are running away from your own death that has brushed past you like many tall ferns in the dark. Your life has no witness but you and, occasionally, your four friends who love you. It is devastating. It is the best day you've ever had. It is the end of the world. You are love itself, and dying.

Reverb Destiny

A man is standing
in the middle
of the freeway
with the traffic
slowing down
around him.
When I pass him,
I see his face.
He is crying.
I don't know why
but I can picture
the reasons:
the chemicals
whispering along
the highway
of my mind, telling me
I deserve my sickness
lurking inside me
like a truck driver
in the cab at a rest stop
in Nebraska
where I pulled over
to listen to thousands
of sandhill cranes
rushing over me.
A silver river
flickering in the sky.
Maybe it's easier
to go away than expect
a person to stay
the same but if I called
you would you say

I'm okay and would I
say I'm clinging
to a different kind
of morning?
                    A dazed walk
and white irises.
Cottontop quail
running on their pin legs.
In Grand Island,
there was an SUV
flipped in a front yard
crushed flat
to the chassis.
The firemen
were standing around
by an ambulance
with its lights off,
children's clothes
spilling out
across the grass.
Hollyhocks
pink as your elbows
on the corner
and roaches
on the sidewalk.
I was following
my grandfather
into a culvert
under the road
until the smell
drove us back out,
the carcass of a deer
melting at the end
of the tunnel,
light slanting

through rib bones.
Heavy raindrops
hitting the pavement
on the other side,
heat lightning
firing in the dusk
glittering up
the sweating
parking lot
where someone says
she got the word
tenacious tattooed
and he got a question mark,
and the genius
of total strangers,
the genius of the truth,
the smell of
a man pouring
Jack Daniels out
his driver-side window.
              Once, you asked me
in tall grass
if there were snakes,
and I said I haven't seen
a snake in years,
and of course
there's the snake,
red as a tongue,
electrified and
darting like a fire
into the dark.
Remember
those billboards
that said if you died tonight
where would you go?

I always thought
it would be right here,
the house
in the summer
smelling minty
like Roundup and paint,
screen door closed
with the front door open,
cold butter
on white bread,
you know
how that tastes.

How to Be a Good Man (If Conditions Are Better to Be a Wildfire)

Buy your friend a beer
with money you don't have.
Make a beautiful omelet
and hold his head in your hand.
Wear a corduroy jacket
under the covers. Do meth
at the roller rink. Be a child
forever (if you're wealthy).
Buy an old pickup truck
on Craigslist. Lose everybody
you've ever loved one
at a time. Feel like the world
is going to kill you and crowd
surf in your work boots.
Remind yourself that love
is something you remind
yourself of. Have appendicitis
and react to death in an embarrassing
way that your friends
will walk in on. Be wronged
egregiously in Durango, Colorado.
Ask yourself if your nipples
are a need or an aesthetic.
Dream about the black worms
all over you in the bathtub.
Eat someone's tongue
with mustard seeds
and pickled carrots
on marrow spread thin.
Be somebody's boy. Buoy.
Bob stupidly among

the golden white bellies of
the upturned boats and
ring-necked doves. Get splashed
with gutter water. Get hailed
on. Dye your hair blonde
even though you are already
blonde. Let your female friends
dress you up like a Ken doll,
and don't kiss any of them.
Become a purse dog of a person.
Wear a shirt that is nonthreatening.
Try on that pair of Wranglers
again. Maybe they'll fit you
if you surprise them.
Come home to one person
in your bed every night
and stay who you are
for the rest of your life.

Out Here You Can Say Anything

You won't notice until you see
the agate alien eyes
of bighorn ewes clustered
on a highway shoulder and you think,
not of their wildness, but of the way
their faces look like your mother
and her sisters standing together
against the tired unknown
of a farmhouse kitchen. Eventually,
your heart will feel flat as an alpine lake
you skip grief across to watch it sink,
nameless. You drove the ocean
of Wyoming while lightning
raked its fingers through the night
the way you pull long bright
hairs off your mother's sweater.
You will wish you could remember
how to cry, standing in the glassy plain
outside Gunnison where it is four degrees
and everything living is crusted with rime
and the sky is white and the ground
is white and the air is white and you rise
up from the asphalt as if born
to the darkness of it alongside
the ravens picking at an elk cow,
her shoulder sloping broken
as the mountains that sat up tall in the dawn
and scooched closer like your mother
leaning into you at the funeral
and when you speak the names of fathers
out loud, a murmuration of swallows
passes over you with the sound

of tearing paper, diamond bellies
shining white, conjured from the air
like snow, like breath.

Simple Divorces

Oklahoma, receive me
my friends
like a storm breaking
into the embrace
of the prairie
into the nights
lasting my whole life
the black road
cut into the golden plain
the black cattle
cut into the golden plain
abandoned telegraph poles
a hundred thousand crosses
on the altar of progress
the veins of red earth
running beneath the grass
Oklahoma, receive me
like the Silver Jews DJ night
a billboard boasting
a $799 cremation
your woman in Topeka
you've never met
who makes batik
tie-dye shirts and who is beautiful
the way someone
who will not drive
is beautiful
living is going to take
back everything
it gave to you
every junkyard
longhorn

every skeletonized
armadillo
every defunct
rattlesnake museum
it takes courage
to do something
as embarrassing
as saying I'd give it up
to get kicked in the nuts
just once
Oklahoma, receive me
away from the oil-
derrick-themed picnic area
outside Dallas
where daffodils are filled
with a billion tiny shards
of glass and if you pick them
the sap can burn your hands
and I picked so many
in New England
like an idiot
from the desert
grinning for the flowers
sprouting up from the cracks
no one warned me
it would hurt
so it didn't
Oklahoma,
Jesus never saw a place
that wasn't a table
never saw a nail
that wasn't waiting
for a hammer
and never felt angry
when they turned on him

together
there are parts of me
I will never see
there are parts
of Louisiana
that are underwater
there are two boats.
and one heart
there's a forest
of mesquite trees
full of the warbles
of quail and wild
pigs ripping holes
in the dirt and
you'll never see it
you're watching
at the snow
turning purple
by the highway
the tractor trailers
black against the gradient
sky flying away
from you with the velocity
of all things and soon
you will eat kaya toast
in the city where you live
under two planets
who are nearly touching
the way we are

Onion Sugar

The smallest bird in North America visits me in my sleep   Landing on
the clock over the doorway in the house I grew up in   August is the
season of dreams   and   Waking up with a hornet in my hand
Black cat with the rotting neck vanishing into air   What I saw before the
heat broke   Caterpillars on tomato vines working to become humming-
bird moths   How much poison did you eat to become   beautiful

Little girls in sisterly bathing suits lying on their backs in puddles of water
beside park bathrooms reflecting   clean sky like a mirror   To a moth
every light is the moon hanging on the horizon   Red as a veined sliver
of peach in a black bowl   Dream-drunk punks in the rain walking on
horses in the summer grass of the plain isn't it   erotic   doesn't it turn
you on   Girl kissing the motorcycle driver   from the jump seat
Boy lifting the girl off of the street   Nicotine lozenge falling out of your
friend's   mouth into his father's hot tub   Sunflowers nodding their
gone-by heads east   This summer it rains with the sun out   I'll
always think of it   Getting cold   on the beach   in Massachusetts
jumping off the pier in a life jacket   The only really good   memory
I have with my mother who for once encouraged me   and   Who did it
herself to prove something   the brine in my mouth and how strong I
was   How inside my body   I could be   My white legs about
to turn ten   Copper bracelet rusting green   I'll think of it   when
it rains in Midland   And in Oregon and Georgia   And California and
Maine and in the street in Reno   when the air is cool as water wrapping
around us   the sun flushing the desert every color of salt

Every Significant Thing I've Ever Done

did you feel it, though?

when the backs of your teeth were numb and

sparkling?   when Paul Simon sang we all shall be received

in Graceland?   when the river clouds grazed the land like the cows

in Kansas?   the gas station toothbrushes

liquor store baseball caps   blown out railroad bridges

blackbirds undulating over the semis

the burning bottomland   the dives with no dancing

you were told no matter what   make sure whoever is stuffing your parachute isn't

wasted   the man in a captain's hat holding the rim

of a trashcan with both hands   like he was steering the ship of Memphis

the devil in a red dress and wire-framed glasses

getting into her Uber outside the bar

the blue rooms where we held each other

snow geese over Atlanta at night   like a lot of loosed gossamer

I woke up crying   you woke up screaming

both of us reticently ripped   into our lives

two beachfront promises   at the edge of an evaporating reservoir

it's so hard to want everything   I don't know if I ever will again

Sex, Blood, Pizza

Two of my friends are in the hospital today: one with COVID
one with head injuries from being attacked because she's trans.

Maybe that is a bad place to start.
No country is worth dying for

but when I imagine leaving mine,
it's like turning my back on my own coffin.

In another life, I could have been a guy
in a band but I'm a guy with a pussy so I have to be complicated instead.

I know I was born
because I was told.

I know I'm American
because of how I was born.

I know you're sad
because you're pretending to have fun.

You're like a fire, making your own weather.
I am a trash bag full of gasoline in the trunk of your car.

When I open up your heart, I find it bookmarked
with a printed-out recipe for tortellini soup.

When I remember the old life, it's the way bubblegum
remembers an extinct banana:

your naked ass in the morning, us faithfully fucking.
Mushrooms kicked apart on the sidewalk.

Tamales for breakfast on a church lawn.
Swamp-cooler smell with rhubarb syrup.

Wearing sandals wherever I wanted
without being worried I'd have to run for it.

I don't know how it happened
but when some guy stuck a needle between my eyes

the only thing I could think was
I am not afraid of pain anymore.

Goddamn Universe

I wanted to live
in this junk drawer
of a city with you
among the pyramids
and piles of ripped up
rebar like wads of hair
from a bristle brush
beside the Mississippi.
A rehabilitation of pigtails
in the constant twilight
of a motel room.
A Sudafed with your
cold brew. I will feel out
how impressive
I want to be today.
Tennessee is a hallway
stretching between
the lottery numbers
in a gas station
and sprays of redbud trees
in some unmarked canyon.
It's important to be honest.
It's important to be
emotional. I'm sorry
if I was bullshitting you
before. I have measured out
my life in Cook Out trays,
the synth in the middle
called insane glory,
the wisteria piled
all over everything
like a beautiful rash

and knowing which NASCAR
drivers died of AIDS.
Life is a rental.
Bad idea in cowboy boots.
You can be a hinge
in the door of reality
and give up
on significance
but I wanted
to write something
so full it felt empty,
an ornate bowl from the past
filled with nothing
but what happened.
I wanted everyone
to tap me in the chest
with the back of a hand
to say goodbye
like men do.
I wanted you to know
I loved you the way
a concrete wall loves
the color of the sky at dusk.
I loved you when you cried
while you sang. It was as easy
as Sunday morning leaving
Athens, where we stayed up
eating curry with the hardcore
band and shouting
about Defiance, Ohio.
It was as hard
as the wet blue linoleum
illuminated by the storm light
in Knoxville. It was invisible
until you couldn't miss it

like the black dog
in the black night
you hit with your ex-
wife's car. It was that time
of day when even the pebbles
have shadows. It was a lot of things
and couldn't save us,
not even sympathetic magic
or rainbow-flag decals,
summer looming
over the ocean
smelling like peaches
rotting off the branch
and never ending.
I would have crossed
state lines for less.

Can I Call You From Waffle House?

You don't have to be the American dream.
You can still walk around drinking a Coke
kind of fucked up and lazy
and right next to the freeway.
I wanted you to come home so bad
I ran to the back door with apple petals in my hair.
I got down on my knees and scrubbed the floor.
The house finches sang from the Christmas lights
and even the real flowers looked plastic.
A heron flew through the legs of tower cranes.
The drought made the trees brittle
and the wind snapped them off.
Do you see the rolling walls of dust
shrouding the horizon, the tractor trailers
tipped on their sides like sleeping
colts one after another? Did you say
your goodbyes inside that bell jar of a forest
to the Mylar balloon fading in the grass,
its vacant smiling reminding you of someone
who remembers the person you used to be
a little too well telling you that the past
doesn't change and the future
is erasing itself the way a fire is erasing
the blazes you watched your father hack
into the trunks of aspens and the sharp
animal smell of cut poplar like the raw side
of a cinch strap on an unworn saddle
the color of the scalloped edges
of a moth's wing as it dies
on wet ash in the all-day dusk of smoke
and rain mixing on some twisting road
as familiar as a touch on the back

of your neck across the truck while Bruce
Springsteen sings, *It wasn't the bitterness*
of the dream that didn't come true,
baby, it was me and it was you
and it was nothing but time and a phone
call while you were trying to sleep.
You might call it a motivation
of queer effervescence to answer
but it's not. I make pozole when I want
to think about the past but I make
a poem to think about the future
and it's an elegy to whatever
this would have looked like
if we had been told sooner
that most of living is here
drinking a beer
and listening to basketball
from the other room. Even
tomorrow, the house will look
the same and your coffee
will taste weaker. If you
want to be reborn, you
have to do it yourself.

But I'll Say It Now

I never said
my favorite night
was when we shot
those dogs together.
You killed the first one
and winged the other.
We walked it down
by its blood
in the moonlight
to the arroyo.
It was winter
and we were men.
The dogs
were expensive
and glossy
like horses discarded
in the dormant reeds. Later
when the lost dog
posters appeared
on the fence posts
up the road
we saw them
and never said a word
just drove by
with our heads fixed
forward.
Blood moon.
Dead dog moon.
My father's moon
silver as cottonwood
leaves dried out
and papering

the ground.
It was the winter
before he helped
pull the body
of a five-year-old girl
out of the willows
where the creek
comes into the river.
It was the winter
after his father died.
He was my father too,
our father who fathered
my father's fatherhood.
I know it eats at you
that you never became him.
It eats me too. You know
people want me to feel
embarrassed
about the way
I grew up,
insist I never loved it
and that I was trying
to escape. If you look back
further, you'll see the top half
of a cat on the doorstep
of the house,
its twisted face
and one arm
left intact.
You'll see
the mother
of the boy

who died in a house
fire in fifth grade
coming to the funeral
with her hair burned off
and her hands bandaged
where she'd lost fingers
searching in the coals.
The diamondback
under the porch
and the big hole I dug
on the far corner
of the property
one summer
when it was so dry
you could dig four feet
and not hit water.
I dug it in a rectangle
and cut down
a half-dead elm
for the roof
which I covered
with sticks and dirt
and grass. I would lie
down there for hours
at the bottom of the hole.
I wasn't a suicidal kid
but I wanted to
come up out of there
and dry out
on a fence post
reborn. My father
buried all our neighbors'
horses because he was the one
with a backhoe
their big loose ankles

draped with a chain
dragged backwards
into oblivion
and dirt. There is
something
down there
trying to get out,
but it can't find the exit
and it thrashes
in the back of my throat,
against my new
Adam's apple.
I'm so sad
I feel sick
and there's nothing
to do for it
like the night
I lay awake
after the surgery
vomiting
and vomiting
alone in the dark
my stomach
splitting open,
but when I looked
it was glued shut
and nothing
happened
except that other hole
in me widened
a little more.
The most masculine thing
you can do is feel empty.
At a certain point,
the world stops

getting bigger.
The weather
becomes more
historic,
and your windows
will ice up
from the inside,
and you'll still
be too hot to sleep.
There's something
very gender-
affirming about
being fucked raw
that I'm not
sure how to explain.
Trust and respect
the masculinity
of not worrying
about consequences.
Being trans is hard,
but being a guy
is so fucking easy.
You can ask
for painkillers,
and no one turns
you down.
I misbehave,
and no one
arrests me. No one
even notices
my innocent
little desires.
I want to get stoned
and watch
that Wim Wenders movie

and touch your cock
over your pants. I want
to wake you
up but in a gay way. I am
a prisoner
of my own good
fortune
the novelty of you
the mutual recognition
of wiping your nose
on your sleeve
and getting caught
by someone
who is also wiping
their nose
on their sleeve.
How many times
have I depended
on a family
being two guys
hanging out?
How many times
can I eat a burrito
at midnight
and lose
at Buck Hunter
and hypothesize
about Mars
in Gemini? How
many pictures
can I take of myself
before I run
out of storage? It's easy
to die. The hard part
is wearing

a dead poet's bolo tie
and finding his name
in books at the used
book store. The hard part
is hanging on
when your grip on life
feels like clenching your
buttcheeks together
for hours. I don't mean
to be unserious
I'm not sure
how else to say it.
The snow
is thin and dry.
There are nuthatches
living in the eaves
of the house
that I scare out
and they flee
to the fir tree
and yell at me
about it while I say
I'm sorry
I'm sorry
it's true
I am hoping
one person in particular
will see my Instagram
stories. It's true
you try to do
what they tell you
and let desire
come into your heart
without judgment
but my heart is big

and dumb
as a dead horse
bloated
on its own longing
and too heavy
to move.
There's nothing
to do but get
a boilermaker
and let the storm
roll in the way
they do
this time of year
fast
like an avalanche
of air
and the trans masc
or butch dyke
bartender will put
their hand
right in the middle
of my back
when they ask
if I want
another one.
You called it
a gay awakening
and I called it
holding you gently
to my chest.
I've learned
the secret
to masculine intimacy
is to be emotionally available
and unembarrassed.

I'd love to crush
a couple beers
and kiss. I'd love
to know how
to write about something
besides men
and leaving. What
is there to say
about Denver?
The mountains?
The freeway?
The prairie fires?
The snow?
They don't plow
the roads
but they will fine you
for not shoveling
your sidewalk.
When I went
home this fall
it was the greenest
I've ever seen it
and my dad
pointed out all the trees
that were beginning to die
right at the top.
Trees I've known
forever
and he tells me
the adobe factory
closed forever
while the steam
walked up
from the river
in the dawn.

He tells me
both my brake lights
are out and to leave
the cars in front of me
a lot of space
in case I get rear-ended.
It's human nature
to take being alive really
fucking personally but
it's also that my life
is a little spray
of iridescent
butterfly scales
up a windshield
and so few people
I know live
this way
but I don't know
anything else. I have to
keep doing these crazed
and wild things
or I will forget
how to feel.
I have just shoveled
the sidewalk.
It is -3 degrees.
The neighbors
were shoveling
their sidewalks too.
Before they took me
into surgery,
I looked
at the ceiling
and thought
that my time

has been good
enough
and it was true
which is funny.
I don't know
when I became
so decisive
and mellow.
I used to be
so keyed up
all the time. I used to
do cocaine
and almost die
now I just hold people
and pet their hair
and let them
admire me. Now
I have a lot to say
about how to live.
I've changed
everything about me
the way
I always wanted
to be changed.
I've written
so many things
about running
away to become
a different person
and then I did it
but I stayed here.

Nothing's Hanging Out Going to Whole Foods.

You can't imagine it: the smell drying onto cardboard & into an old
Red wheelbarrow full of stomachs heavier & whiter than the moon. They do not
Do that where you are from. Where you are from, a velvet rope runs the circumference
Of death & you stood in line with a ticket just to touch it. Your mother told the school
You had the flu. Where you are from, we longed to have each other's orgasms & we ate
Pineapple from Whole Foods under a sky fractured by crabapple blossoms.
Where you are from, there is a guy golfing into a bedsheet hanging in the garage.
He is your father. In the dream, my father puts a tie on me & ties it
Even though neither of us has ever worn a tie in my life.
I make a shitty person, but I would have been an amazing tree,
Filling these astringent hours before dark with a dozen spotted towhees
In my branches above the snow in the backyard that is unmoving & deep
As this new shadow cupping my face. It's not that I want to feel
Nothing, I want to do nothing but feel. They discontinued
Chiclets in 2016 & I didn't even notice them disappearing
From around Our Lady of Guadalupe, different colored squares
That tasted identical: citrus for an instant & then
Nothing. Chops are $9 a pound & most of it is bone.
There was a two-horned ram that split my hand slamming
Through the catch gate I held closed, not suspecting the herd
Could release an individual, one who wanted to live desperately, the way I did.

Can You Take It

mysterious white-tiled houses of childhood lavender outside
he waited apple grafted to a pear tree stuck himself with a needle
a hundred needles the give of skin tight like incense and vinegar
indigo boiling green shake it loose to get the sky inside it
suck it from his fingernails smooth comfort tight like weft
black widow beneath the kiddie pool accumulation
of little despairs bus with the sunset inside it and the eye
are speaking to each other rotting Naugahyde and plastic
mouse piss moth piss red lightning over the mesa
membrane of a rabbit's ear didn't the moon feel closer flat
on his back stolen stop sign damming the acequia
standing water a mirror for the calliope broken
by grass pollen clinging to wet jeans baby crying
in the first house he can remember crying inside of
he's grown now thinking I wish I could cry like
that he was never supposed to remember why he is nothing
but longing they don't touch him anymore they don't have to
Española Chimayó Hernandez Cordova Truchas
Santa Clara Pojoaque Arroyo Seco San Luis Rinconada
El Guache Alcalde La Mesilla San Pedro the world turned over
before sleep smooth comfort like a river stone afraid
of what was not there fire and absence dream
of the lightning field ozone in the dark cottonwood

cotton   in the brown grass   bear   carcass balding   in
the clay   drought as a mother   asking her   son to pack
her suitcase   after leaving   forever   nighthawk   last
companion   to solitude   sensitive child waiting   on
the porch   masa burning   inside   anything is possible
when there is   nothing   squeeze a cattail   so it bursts
brown-and-white fur   dripping   coyote   hanging   dead
in barbed wire   sweet datura   and rot   tanager   and
oriole   leopard frogs   in the old pond   migrating   box
turtle tractoring   to the river   abscess   inside   the deaf
dog's   eye   boys   hit each other   with sticks
until his hands   stung   dared to   grab the electric
fence   his teeth   split his own   tongue   in front
of the geldings   split   his own knuckles   on stucco just for
attention   blue-flax   eyes   holding   water   he waited
lavender and   sage   sewn into linen   rotten heart
of the apricot tree   pears   drying on untreated   pine
the memory   lanolin   and lye   big hands   that
used to do   anything   for him   are now his   when
he looks   down   didn't it feel   thinner   as if
he could pass   between   old   eyes in a lamb's   face
irises fading   into fists   green   meteor   howling over
the back   pasture promising   nothing

Smile, If You'd Like To

I couldn't hold
down a job
when I had one.
I am always trans first
and a person second
but once in a while
I'm allowed to be
nothing at all. Maxx
with two Xs said
people are infinite
while his fingers
were inside me.
People are small
and tired. Angels
came down
from Paradise
after the fire
broken as an old heron
in the road. The boy
from middle school
never made the farm
team and works
for the Department
of Transportation.
I'm sick of coping.
I don't want to be
brave, I want to be happy,
goddammit. I want to live
a full life, you motherfuckers.
Something's wrong.
The cockroach
up my leg in the night,

the lightning storm
we snuck into like kids
on the floor of God's casino,
girls in Reno struggling
to pick each other up
off the tile after the bar
was empty, the man who fell
and cracked his face open
on the patio asking his server
are you going to take care
of me or let them
take me away? Who do you
become when you
are rejected by the world
until you reject yourself?
When you're gone,
you won't remember.
I have that feeling again,
the one where you have a cold
but you're also drunk. Really
nasty but impervious.
I'll lie here and think
about how dumb I am
until I fall asleep. Tomorrow,
I'll write a poem,
which is a machine
that does nothing. I want
to stop thinking
about how I'd do it
if I offed myself
to get out of surviving,
if I had a car accident

to get off work, if I had
another drink to get out
of my head, if I keep
pretending it isn't happening
to feel okay with the future.
I can open my eyes
toward the sky for it
to fall in and out of me
but the closest I've been
was the moon passing
behind the turning
wing of a cloud
the way a finger might
pass over the empty aperture
of a snail's shell, the light
on the birches painting
a thousand wrists white.

The Most Punk Thing You Can't Remember

I dreamed I was never so lonely
Re-treading the years where I have never been
My life saved by a peach sno-cone the color of roses
And sitting on the sidewalk outside the 76 eating fried chicken.
From here I can see where the fire jumped the highway and kept going.
I was so angry I couldn't remember anything about Asheville. My memory
As thin as glass for what I used to be. I had never once given up
On love before it gave up on me. I'm not the type to cut and run.
Someone tells me men's jeans have deep pockets and I say
I know, I'm wearing them too. Where do you go when you're a loser
With bleached hair? The next time we're in Sandusky, Ohio, you'll get us
The jacuzzi suite and the next time I wake up in New Jersey, I'll make sure
You're never hungry again. When it comes down to it, do you
Mourn the people who will be lost or do you feel anxiety for the art
That will no longer have anyone to look at it? Who will
Read my poems when everyone is dead? I dream again
Of the woman I was. I see her across the room more clearly
Than I have ever seen myself awake and she looks really good
And there was never anything wrong with her but she couldn't stay.
Where can I stay? The unpruned orchards out by Buffalo, the trees
Twisted as silver hands, heavy with years of fruit. The blackbirds streaming
Into the last hour of sun. The green glass insulators gleaming
On telephone poles, the veal kennels backlit on the hills
With little steers silhouetted inside them doing all they will ever do
Which is sit down or stand up. Where is there to go? Do you feel
This slow shattering everywhere too? The high horsefeather clouds and all our
Hearts wobble like a few windows left in a burned-out house.

I Know What I'm Doing and Why

It's one of those nights
I think I want a beer
but I actually want
a different life.
The guy at the liquor store
looks like my dad.
He tells me to drink
cold water for my hiccups
and I'm birthed out
into traffic. Cicadas
in the hot wind. Airplanes
constellating. The moon
red and rising. Birds
in the bedroom
and new blacktop
steaming in the street.
Laugh like a sob. Drinking
like punctuation in a paper bag.
It's bad. On the bus
a woman asks
if I'm reading psalms.
I laugh like a laugh
and say no it's poetry
and she says you look
like the daughter
of a woman
at Christ the King.
I say no I'm a saint
of the poet church
where everyone's a saint.
I get off the bus alone
walking the darkness as a man.

Body, a pegboard
to hang anger on
beside the hammers
in the garage.
Body, a bathtub
a wall socket
an earring
kicked under the radiator.
Three titted mannequins
undressed in a storefront.
Skin like a peeled apple.
Somewhere I heard
the children of people
who didn't want kids
become lonely adults
and I'm so fucking lonely, Mom.
Late summer goes on forever
with your late twenties
and the little hairs
on peaches are God's pubes.
Monarch wings fluttering
where they're stuck
to the windshield. A guy
on the 101 overpass
unleashing a Coca-Cola-
colored fountain
of puke over the guard rail.
Pines unknitting
along the road
in Humboldt County.
Your nephew eating
the fried off his chicken.

The thing about not belonging
anywhere is you don't have
anything to miss
so you miss everything
without knowing
what you're missing.
Redwoods grow
straight out
of the stumps
of their parent trees.
The oysters we ate
on the coast tasted
like the sunset
air off the water. There
was toilet paper
stringing the flowers
and you cried
when we saw the ocean
from the road.
I need a way to say
I was raised as a body
and had to become a person
or I want to want to live
among the detritus of dislike
mushrooms and baby corn
picked out of lo mein
in the biggest parking lot
for the biggest military
in history.
I will be the
designated stranger
standing out here
and looking in.

Little Dog Day

Horchata in a styrofoam cup.
Oil derricks nodding
Inside city limits.
Subdivision houses flimsy
As lady fingers.
I can't wait to find
A dry place to sit down.
If you're from America,
I don't think you can
Ever understand it
Although maybe that's
Giving too little credit
To fish in the water.
It's less about riding
The bronc and more the moment
Before the chute opens.
A country is a condition
Under which we are allowed
To give that cowboy nod
And start the clock but not
Whether we want to hurt or
Be hurt and it does
Hurt everybody.

How to Be a Wildfire (If Conditions Are Better to Be a Man)

Text your glamorous friend
in their better city something
incriminating and selfish.
Buy a vibrator with your
royalties. Prefer men
to landscapes. Listen
to that Joni Mitchell record
with the big scratch
on the B-side. Live inside
the scratch. Believe that
everyone who loves
you is a better person
than you. Try to sink.
Try to drain. Spool
apart like honey
in a homemade
centrifuge. Wrestle
your sister to the ground
until the neighbors
call the cops. Stay
home from the house
party. Spend your
birthday hangover
looking for the naked guy
with the infected lotus
tattoo. Find him
strung out under
your roommate's mom's
crocheted quilt
on the living room
floor. See the same band

fifteen times. Wear
your friend's slip dress.
Snort ketamine off
her fist. Laugh when
someone who saw your
tits ten years ago says
he'll miss them. Remember
that a fluke is a worm
or the man who was killed
by a deer that ran
through the plate-
glass door of the bus
he was driving and kicked
him to death in his
seat belt. Be told you
will forget everything.
Remember it
anyway. Become
angelic in your
hospital bed. Feel
left out when the hawks
circling you speak
to each other. Return
to your body like a wasp
into the vinegar trap.
Learn to love this,
the only thing you'll
own forever.

Super Bloom

I.

We invent new mothers
in response to absence

or some kind of longing
to be the river

blue-jean blue
like my sister's eyes.

I am a pinched nerve
in the hand of the world.

I want to brush my cheek
against this sick and dying

forest the way my friend pets his elderly dog.
We were not meant to outlive the trees.

The antelope sitting in the sun
blushing their pale hair

fleshy and human in the wintering grass.
The only other animals you'll see

out here are someone else's horses
and a northern harrier

flying low over the Dollar Tree
and the snake

on the don't tread on me hat
of the gas station attendant

moving so slowly he seems
nearly holy handing you your change

and your friend
who is shivering

on the corner
in their jean jacket

under the budding magnolias
in the streetlights

where we'll rest our knees
against other knees beneath a bar top.

II.

The rain
and the sun

and the ocean
and the asphalt

steaming where it runs
over secret green pools

covered in lily pads
the color of the electric

yellow moss racing up
every tree trunk

and someone you used to love
is playing Chopin nocturnes on guitar.

Even when you're scared
art is no dictionary

where the sand becomes the sky
and the ocean becomes a great

white wall and you will walk
on water toward it

past the clam diggers sprinting
up the beach with their wagons

to be the first ones at the back doors
of restaurants in town.

Art is no dictionary
for money.

I mistake the ocean
for traffic noise

at the receding hairline
of the forest.

III.

Time Marches On
in an off-season diner

where a surprised man hadn't heard
they still make Rainier Beer

and I hadn't heard
the frogs

and the rain
and the ocean

and later eating salty mango
sticky rice in bed with you

or The National
in the hail storm

or the whispering snow
in the Cascades

the kindness
of the Portland bartender

who only charged me for one beer
because I was crying

the neighbor proud
of his yellow house

and daffodils saying
I see you seeing them.

I drink water out of my hands
over a dark sink in Eugene

the night the angry boy
with one earring

and cuffed jeans
dedicated a song to me

which sounded like the Red
Hot Chili Peppers but gay.

How can I hold it all
the delicate egg shell of my skull?

The poppies buried in the grass
at the ends of rows of rice.

Everyone looks
more beautiful in California

the light cutting
golden through the smog

and the mist
the penstemons jangling

in the vineyards beneath the strange
and twisted trees

the waves of grass
turning white under the sun

the way a raven's wing
will whiten reflecting pure light

fennel waving in the cracks
of the highway shoulder

hogs in the ditch
with the calla lilies

poppies the color
of citrus peels

twisting shut
for the night

the honey guy
packing up his cattle dogs

and his credit cards
accepted sign.

IV.

In a California I will
never see again

the Torch Club
is packed out

and Marina hugs me
and men who are crying

hug me as fathers
and brothers I'll never know

San Francisco
from the bridge

and ice flowers
cupping invasively

toward the sun
rainbows flashing

in the sharecropped
sprinklers

the crescent moon
and the stars

and the ocean
and Leonard Cohen singing

it don't matter how you worship
as long as you're

down on your knees
and you remember

your friend realizing
you both say both

with an L and the way
he hugged you goodbye

so desperately
and whispered

he loved you
with a smile

and you bolth love
Leonard Cohen

and David Berman and all
the men who are perfectly sad

and who love people
the way you love

the beekeeper cutting
the swarm of honey bees

off an orange tree
into a cardboard box

by the pool at the Motel 6
in San Luis Obispo

his smile when they fall
without sound

and he closes the box
forever in your memory.

V.

Weedy yellow flowers
ripping across

the lowlands of San Diego
where the ocean

touches the desert
which touches

the cranes
over San Bernardino

where there's a couple fighting
and making out between cars

at the gas station
and the ghost

of the moon over
Yermo and the hills

of the Mojave
sloping like the soft

piebald udders
of jenny donkeys

nursing their foals
among the cactus

blossoms in the shadow
of a billboard for Terrible's.

When I die
it will be murder.

There is no proof
that the world

did not love me
did not offer me

the empty beach
with black sand and purple sky

or the pouting
mouths of poppies

or the discarded sunlight
on my friend's favorite

plaster hot dog
fading over the 7-Eleven

and did not show me
that seeds will wait

a decade for the rain
the way my father

showed me a gallon box
of warm strawberries

from the side of the road
outside Fresno once

when I was ten years old
and I stood in the dust

and ate them until my fingers
were red and we walked

to the oasis of a Safeway
for Reddi-Wip because it's true

you can make a good thing
better if you ask.

Everybody is a mirror
whether they know it or not

and there is no proof
I did not love the world too.

You Love My Old Ways

I died once before
but I had no idea
I was going to get old.
Rusted-out sky
for the pelvis
of the country
where my existence
was denied. The wrong
name on a grave. Butterfly
kite in the crabapple tree.
The years balled up in socks.
If I didn't have bad luck,
I'd have no luck at all.
A woman as blonde
as her dog looked at me
from the gap. She spray-
painted her belt black.
Ankle tattoo of a dragon
above Adidas Sambas
talking about her alien beliefs.
Would you break the law
for those you love? Guns,
saints, drugs, my manhood
a Learjet rotting on a lawn
in Tennessee. Barefoot
woman and a dead pony
on the side of the road.
She says Elvis was one
of the last men
who mattered,
extinct with the Carolina
parakeet. I drenched

myself in Memphis.
I mean the mud.
The mud might glitter.
If you never look
over your shoulder,
the future will not arrive.
It's a little on the nose
like vultures
on a ruined house.
Like turning swastikas
into hearts in the stalls
of the Love's bathroom.
Like vomiting pale
green foam
into the magnolias
on the streets
of New Orleans.
Up north, they are burning
the forests of Mississippi.
Ghosts ambling
in the smoke. Scruffy
cows posted up
under the pylons.
Crimson clover spilled
across the embankments
like all beautiful blood.
Fishing rods and F150s.
I have given up on context.
You don't need me to tell you.
The killing of the world
is the absence
of responsibility.

You play hard because
every other touch
has to be soft. Sublimate
your anguish, hemmed up
in the honeycomb
of railroad ties.
The only righteous thing
you can do as an American
is die but if you don't want anything
larger than a blade of grass
to cut through you,
lay the fuck down.
This is the demon
of joking around.
I try to say goodbye
and the train sobs.
Maybe if I hadn't met myself
somewhere else, maybe
if my heartbreak
hadn't been my own body,
I never would have
heard it, on the porch
in my underwear, long night
of Arkansas, moon
setting crescent as two thorns
in the honeysuckle,
and the roaring
coming from nowhere
and everywhere,
the sound of my life
with my boots on backwards.

Acknowledgments

"Little Dog Day" was first published in *Protean Magazine.*

"Every Significant Thing I've Ever Done" was first published in *HAD.*

"The Thing No One Wants You to Know" was first published in *Peach Mag.*

"Out Here You Can Say Anything" was first published in *Sprung Formal.* The title is taken from Larry Levis's *Winter Stars.*

"The Most Punk Thing You Can't Remember" was first published in *MAYDAY.*

"Nothing's Hanging Out Going to Whole Foods" and "Sex, Blood, Pizza" were first published in *Afternoon Visitor.*

"I Know What I'm Doing and Why," "How to Be a Good Man (When Conditions Are Better to Be a Wildfire)," "Onion Sugar," and "Can I Call You from Waffle House?" were first published in *the tiny.*

"How to Be a Wildfire (When Conditions Are Better to Be a Man)" was first published in *Voicemail Poems.*

"Simple Divorces" was first published in Sundress Press's *Transmasculine Poetics Anthology.*

"Goddamn Universe" was first published in *no tokens.*

Thank you to Mike Young for helping me put this book together and for being the love of my life.

Thank you to Sommer Browning for all your light.

Thank you to my dad and my mom and EJ and Anne and Red.

Thank you to Isadora Decker-Lucke, Sumner Erhard, Angus Smith, Colin Sheehan, Megan Ellsworth, Adam Cabrera, Riley Marino, Alec Doniger, Dave Knodle, Olivia Shaw, Willi Carlisle, Dick Darden, Dylan Earl, Jude Brothers, Eryn Brothers, Will Mulligan, Evan Jeffers, Nate Smerage, Vaughn Mims, Jake DeMarco, Mia Soza, Amie Bradley, Sierra Cicada, Wes and Molly Hamilton, Marty Eichenauer, Dan Campbell, and everyone else who has brought the music to the poetry.

Thank you to Peter Gizzi, Dara Barrois-Dixon, Lindsey Webb, Kylan Rice, Caroline Rayner, G.D. Harkavy, Alex Benke, Zoe Tuck, Emily Hunderwadel, Mathias Salvina, Christopher Payne, Amanda Dahill-Moore, Rachelle Toarmino, Will Erickson, Tony Mancus, Blake Butler, and all the other writers who have held me and helped me over the years. Thank you to Jordan Stempleman and Ebs Sanders for soliciting poems from this book to publish.

Gion Davis is a trans poet from Española, New Mexico, where he grew up on a sheep ranch. His poetry has been featured in *HAD, No Tokens, Sprung Formal, the tiny,* and other publications. His debut collection, *Too Much* (2022), was selected by Chen Chen for the 2021 Ghost Peach Press Prize. For the past four years, he has toured and performed with the DIY music collective Clementine Was Right, and his contributions to songwriting have been highlighted in publications such as *Paste* and *Stereogum*. He graduated with his MFA in Poetry from the University of Massachusetts Amherst in 2019 and currently lives in Denver, Colorado.